MW00939340

The No-Fluff Guide to Writing Web Content:

From articles to blog posts, all the information you need without any fluff.

Contents

Introduction

As a freelance writer for more than 20 years, I've seen some stuff. Rough, sad web content in the form of articles and blog posts that leave the reader with a zero. Nothing to take away except boredom and questions.

That pains me.

Your audience should get exactly what they came for!

So, I put together this book. It contains my best tips for writing awesome content, and even some tips for building your brand as a writer.

My goal is to build you up with the knowledge you need to go out into the online world and dazzle potential clients and readers, alike.

Enjoy, my No-Fluffers!

Alina Bradford, The No-Fluff Writer

Chapter 1: How to Write a Paragraph the Right Way

Let's start out with the basics. Writing a paragraph is one of the simplest parts of writing.

No doubt you can write a sentence, that's easy. The problem comes when you try to lace those sentences together to make a paragraph, and then go on to write another paragraph.

No matter if you're just starting out as a writer, or have some experience under your belt, this chapter will get your work read and published. Sit back and take notes.

The First Line

There are several types of paragraphs. The type of paragraph you're writing determines what your opening sentence will be. Types of paragraphs include:

An introduction paragraph- These are found at the beginning of a blog or article and are meant to draw the reader in while giving them a pretty firm idea of what the rest of the paragraphs are about.

Think of it as a hey-I've-got-something-awesome-for-you-so-here's-a-little-summary paragraph. Hit them with an interesting fact or statistic. Try to get this done in three to four sentences. Be sure to use your keyword as soon as possible, too.

Example:

"40 percent of writers don't know how to write a paragraph correctly, according to Writing XYZ Magazine. That's a shocking statistic, but you may be in that percentage and not even know it. Here's what you need to know so that you're not part of the clueless masses."

Standard paragraph- The first line of a standard paragraph is meant to either introduce the reader to a topic or to continue a thought from the last paragraph.

Closing paragraph- A closing paragraph sums up what your post was about and tells the reader what to do next. This can be encouraging the reader to click on a link to an article, book, item you're selling, whatever. No matter what you guide your reader to next, this bit is called a Call to Action (CTA).

Inside the Paragraph

Once you have the opening sentence down, there are a few rules you need to follow.

First, don't repeat the main word in every line. For example:

Wrong: "40 percent of writers don't know how to write a paragraph correctly, according to Writing XYZ Magazine. That's a shocking statistic about writers, but you may be in that percentage and not even know it. Here's what you need to know so that you're not part of the clueless writer's club."

Notice I used the word "writers" in every sentence. That's bad. Not only does it make the paragraph boring, writing the same word over and over again will hurt the article's SEO (we'll talk more about SEO later). Break out your thesaurus and use synonyms when you can.

For example, here's some words that can replace writer in the sample paragraph:

- Word wranglers
- Scribes
- Author, journalist, poet, blogger, columnist (depending on what type of writer you're talking about)

Next, be sure that each sentence is different. Using sentences that are the same length is boring. Mix it up.

Use:

- A short sentence
- A compound sentence (a sentence that uses 'and,' 'or,' 'but,' 'though,' a semicolon or a colon, etc.)
- A sentence that uses a comma
- Quotes
- Statistics

You get the idea. Sentence salad. Just make sure that each sentence makes sense in how it connects to the sentence before it. Using different lengths of sentences, but not making them work together in a harmonious stream of thought isn't going to work.

Check out the difference between these two paragraphs:

Writing is fun. It takes work. Keep being creative. Use variety. Keep readers entertained.

Writing is fun, but it takes work. Keep being creative. Use variety to keep readers entertained.

Thought the first paragraph is perfectly fine, it's boring and choppy because it only used super short sentences. Mixing up the sentence structures made the paragraph more interesting.

Finally, be sure to always transition from one paragraph to the next. You can do this by using transitional words in the first sentence. These words continue the thought from the last paragraph.

Some transitional words and phrases include:

- 'First,' 'second,' and 'third'
- Next
- Finally
- Again
- Also
- Then
- Though
- Additionally
- On the other hand
- Remember
- Don't forget
- Conversely
- Even though
- Not only
- Actually
- Besides
- Likewise
- Hence
- Thus
- Later
- Immediately
- Meanwhile
- Therefore
- Consequently
- For instance
- For example
- Of course
- Otherwise

- Still
- Yet
- In contrast

Take a look back at my previous paragraphs in this chapter and you'll see I use transitional words a lot. They help your reader follow your thought process. Transitional words are particularly useful for guiding readers through how-to instructions.

Bullet Points and Numbered Lists

A great way to make your work easy to read is by breaking paragraphs down into numbered or bulleted lists. There are some rules about using these lists properly, though.

First, use numbered lists when you're explaining steps of a how-to or project to your reader. Also, make sure you don't start each step start with a transition word. Your numbers are doing that for you.

Right:

1. Pour the batter into the bowl.
2. Add ½ cup of milk.
3. Stir until the batter starts to bubble.

Wrong:

1. First, pour the batter into the bowl.
2. Next, add ½ cup of milk.
3. Finally, stir until the batter starts to bubble.

Use bulleted lists when you have a list of items or points. For example, say I was writing an article about monkeys and wanted to make a list of foods they like to eat. My bulleted list would look something like this:

- Fruits
- Nuts
- Seeds
- Flowers

Notice that in the numbered list I used punctuation and in the bulleted list I did not? The rule is that if you're writing a full sentence, use punctuation in your list. If you are just listing an item, skip the punctuation.

The first word in your numbered or bulleted lists must always be capitalized, though. There's no budging on that one.

Pro tip: Make sure your lists don't start with the same word. Mix it up.

Right:

1. Click the right button.
2. Scroll to the Start menu and select it.
3. Choose the program from the list.

Wrong:

1. Click the right button.
2. Click the Start menu.
3. Click on the program from the list.

Get Your Paragraph's Spelling and Grammar Right

Top-notch writing skills are a necessity to make a living as a writer, of course. The English language is tricky business, however, and remembering all the rules can be hard.

Never fear!

This list of dozens of easy-to-remember tricks will help you improve your spelling and grammar, giving your writing skills the polish they need.

Passive or Active Voice

Do you have a hard time figuring out the difference between passive and active voice? Try this trick: Add the phrase **"by zombies"** to the end. If it still makes sense, it's passive voice. So "She was carried away" is passive, because "She was carried away by zombies" would make sense.

What's a Preposition?

Not sure what a preposition is? It's anything a squirrel can do to a tree: it can go up a tree, it can go down a tree, it can go in a tree or out a tree or around a tree... All those words—**up, down, in, out, around—are prepositions**.

Sit vs. Set vs. Lay vs. Lie

Sit, set, lay and lie are confused a lot. Basically, sit and lie are used when someone is getting comfortable. They both have an "I" so use that to remember that they are used for a person or some type of living being. For example, you tell a child to sit, not set.

Set and lay are used when something is being placed somewhere. They both need an object in the sentence. For example, "I set my glass down on the table."

Desert or Dessert?

A desert is a dry, arid plot of land, while dessert is a delicious morsel of food often enjoyed after dinner. If you struggle to keep the two separated in your head, just remember this:

Dessert has 2 Ss because you want more and more of it.

Principle or Principal?

A principle is a basis for a belief in something, while a principal is the head of a school. The old rule is just to remember **your principal is your pal.**

How Do You Spell Cemetery?

Struggling to remember how to spell cemetery? Remember that **it has 3 Es—like in the word Eeek!**

My Brother and I or My Brother and Me

My brother and I went to the store together—or was it my brother and me? If you're pairing yourself with another person and aren't sure which to say, take the other person out first.

You would never say "Me went to the store"—you'd say "I went to the store"—so in that case, it would be "My brother and I." On the other hand, you *would* say "She let me borrow her car," so for that one, it would be "She let my brother and me borrow her car."

Coordinating Conjunctions

Coordinating conjunctions are words that can be used after commas to link two independent clauses together. To remember your coordinating conjunctions, just remember the acronym **FANBOYS: F**or **A**nd **N**or **B**ut **O**r **Y**et **S**o.

Decimate Defined

Most people think the word "decimate" means to completely destroy something. The key to the actual definition lies in the root word— "deci"—like "decimal" or "decibel." **Decimate, by definition, actually means to reduce something by one tenth.**

Less or Fewer

Not sure when to use less or fewer? Less is when you're talking about something not quantifiable by a number, while fewer is used when you're talking about something you could count. So, for example, grocery store signs should say, "14 items or fewer," not "14 items or less," because you can count how many items in your cart.

Note that the distinction between less and fewer is if you can count something, not if you would want to count something. So you would say, "I would like the beach to have less sand," or you could say, "I would like the beach to have fewer *grains* of sand"—because while you *wouldn't* count all the grains of sand at the beach, grains of sand are something that can be counted, while sand, on its own, is not.

Do or Make

Do you do housework or make housework? Of the two, "do" is an active verb, so here's the test you use: Does it feel like work? If the answer is yes, you use the word "do." Otherwise, you use the word "make."

So, you would do housework, but you would make friends. **Another test is creation. If you're creating something, use make. If you're doing something, use do.**

Adjectives vs. Adverbs

Adjectives and adverbs are both description words. The difference between the two? Adjectives describe nouns while adverbs describe verbs. **One easy trick to remember is that adverbs often end in "ly"—like quickly or stealthily—while** most of your other description words, like purple or sly, are adjectives.

Good vs. Well

When someone asks how you are, do you say, "I'm doing good" or do you say, "I'm doing well?" Believe it or not, there's a difference. **The word "good" has a moral basis to it, whereas the word "well" has to do with how you're feeling.**

So, if you say, "I'm doing good," what you're actually saying is that you're doing something morally good—charity work, for example—whereas if you say you're doing *well*, you mean you're not ailing in any way.

Misplaced Modifiers

Modifiers should always go next to the subject they're modifying, but we misplace them in language all the time. When you're trying to check your writing for this, just remember that **mechanics don't leak oil.**

What does that mean? Consider the following sentence: "Leaking oil, the mechanic fixed the car."

What that sentence is saying is that the *mechanic* is leaking oil, though clearly it should be the car that is leaking oil. So, it should read: "Leaking oil, the car was fixed by the mechanic."

Always Compare Apples to Apples

Have you heard the phrase "comparing apples to oranges?" What this means is that you need to make sure that when you are comparing two items, they're actually equivalent.

Consider this sentence: **The novels of Ernest Hemingway are shorter than William Faulkner.** This is comparing Ernest Hemingway's novels to William Faulkner, not to William Faulkner's novels.

When comparing items in a sentence, you may need to make the sentence longer to be sure you're comparing apples to apples. The sentence above, for example, should read, "The novels of Ernest Hemingway are shorter than the novels of William Faulkner," to avoid confusion.

Affect vs. Effect

Struggling to remember the difference between affect and effect? **Just remember that A is for action.** Affect is a verb form of influence and means "to have an impact on."

For example, you would say "Do you think the weather will affect the turn-out at tomorrow's cook out?"

Effect, on the other hand, is the *result* of an action. For example, you would say "His new airbrushing technique gave his work a cool effect."

What Are Transitions?

Transitions are words that lead you from one idea to the next. **They literally make a transition.** You need these words to guide your reader from one word to the next.

Its vs. It's

Can't keep its and it's straight? Just remember that **it's is longer because it's really two words: It is.** So, if you can replace the word with "it is", then you need the version with the apostrophe. If not, it is the word to us.

Then vs. Than

Then versus than is easy to remember when you keep in mind that **then has an E because it describes eons of time.** For example, "I liked being a kid; things were easier back then."

Than, on the other hand, is a comparison word. For example, "This tree is smaller than your tree."

I.e. vs. E.g.

I.E. and E.G. are both abbreviations of Latin words, and once you know what they're abbreviations of, it's much easier to use them correctly. **I.e. stands for "Id Est" which means "In other words."**

It's used when restating an idea, usually as a way to simplify it. e.g. stands for "Exempli Gratia" and means "For example."

I Before E

We've all heard the phrase "I before E except after C," but sometimes we forget that there's a second part to this rhyme. The full rhyme is **"I before E except after C, or in sounding as 'A' as in Neighbor or Weigh." And don't forget, the word "weird" is weird.**

Stationery vs. Stationary

If you mix these two words up, just remember that **"E" is for "Envelopes" while "A" is for "Automobiles."** So, if you're talking about the paper you'd stick in an envelope, it's stationery. If you're talking about being stuck in your car and not moving, you're stationary.

How to Spell Because

Struggling to spell because? Remember this mnemonic device: "Big Elephants Always Upset Small Elephants."

How to Spell Necessary

Sometimes it's hard to remember if necessary has one C and 2 Ss or 2 Cs and one S. **A helpful way to remember is you can have *one* collar and *two* socks.**

Practice vs. Practise

Mixing up these two words? Remember that practise is a verb with an "S" for "sport," while practice with a "C" is the noun.

How to Spell Rhythm

Trying to remember how to spell rhythm? Remember this mnemonic device: "Rhythm helps your two hips move."

How to Spell Island

When you're remembering how to spell island, remember than an island *is land* with water all around.

Piece vs. Peace

Mixing up piece and peace? Just remember that you want a *pie*ce of pie.

Lose vs. Loose

Lose is to misplace, so it misplaced an O. Loose, on the other hand, is not too tight, so it has room for an extra O.

What's a Semicolon?

Despite its name, a semicolon shouldn't be used to replace a colon. In fact, it's used to replace a period, separating two closely related sentences.

Quotations

Here's a quick and easy rule about quotations: Punctuation always stays inside. So even if you're ending a sentence with a quote, the period would go on the inside of the quotation marks, not the outside.

The only exception is when you have a quote inside of a sentence that ends with and question mark and the quote doesn't. For example: When someone asks how you are, do you say, "I'm doing good" or do you say, "I'm doing well"?

Who vs. Whom

Not sure if you should use who or whom? Rephrase the statement as a question, and then answer it with either "he" or "him." If your answer is "he," then you want the word "who."

If your answer is "him," then you want the word "whom." E.g.: Matt is the one _____ we saw. Who did we see? We saw *him*.

So, it would be "Matt is the one *whom* we saw." Matt is the one _____ went first. Who went first? *He* did. So, it would be "Matt is the one *who* went first."

That vs. Who/Whose/Whom

Not sure if you should use "that" or some form of "who?" *That* is an object word, while *who* is for people. **If you remember that who is for who-mans (humans), you'll be using the words correctly.**

How to Spell Tomorrow

If you struggle to remember how to spell tomorrow, **remember that it used to be two words: To and Morrow, as in, "Let's keep going to the morrow."**

Over time, it was hyphenated into to-morrow, and finally combined to the form we know today — tomorrow.

How to Spell Separate

The middle part of the word "separate" can be hard to keep track of. To remember it, **remind yourself that an R *separates* two As.**

How to Spell Embarrass

It can be hard to keep track of how many Rs and Ss are in the word embarrass. The mnemonic device can help: **"I get [R]eally [R]ed when my [S]ister [S]ings."**

How to Spell Horror

Think of the word "horror" as having two Os because you have to keep your eyes open in fear.

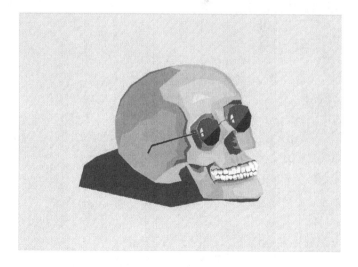

How to Spell Special

Special is spelled with a CIA, because the CIA has Special Agents.

Comma Usage

Here's a fun mnemonic to remember how to use commas: **"A cat has claws at the end of its paws. A comma's a pause at the end of a clause."**

Double Negatives

Double negatives are not grammatically correct, and when you do use them, the two negatives end up countering each other, often saying the opposite of what you intended. Here's an easy saying to help you remember: **"I don't know nothing about double negatives."**

What's an Interjection?

Here's a cute little poem to help you remember what an interjection is: ***"An interjection cries out, "Hark!" I need an exclamation mark!"***

How to Spell Exaggerate

To remember that exaggerate has two Gs, remember that **"Goofy Greg loves to exaggerate."**

How to Spell Difficulty

Struggling to remember how to spell difficulty? Wrestle up some memories of the old *Matilda* movie and say to yourself what the kids said in that movie: **Mrs. D, Mrs. I, Mrs. F. F. I., Mrs. C, Mrs. U, Mrs. L.T.Y.**

How to Spell Environment

Remember that a new environment will *Iron Me* out to get the middle letters in that word in the right order.

How to Spell Truly

Because "truly" is spelled differently than its root word, true, it can be hard to remember how to spell it. Here's a little phrase that will remind you: **"It is *truly* hot in *July*."** Though they're pronounced differently, this can help you remember that truly and July are spelled similarly.

Quite vs. Quiet

Can't remember which word you're trying to use? Remember this little phrase: "It is [Q]uite [U]nbelievably [I]mpossible [T]o [E]njoy Spelling Difficult Words."

How to Spell Vacuum

When you're trying to remember how to spell "vacuum," remember the phrase **"I See Two Ewes in the Field."** That will help you remember that there is 1 C and 2 Us.

Compliment vs. Complement

Trying to remember the difference between compliment and complement? Remember that the opposite of a comp*li*ment is an insult, while when something comp*le*ments something else, it enhances it in some way.

Capital vs. Capitol

A capital, with an A, is a city where main government offices are. A capitol, with an O, is the building where laws are made. To remember the difference, remember that many capitols have domes, both of which have Os.

Weather vs. Whether

Trying to remember whether to use the word weather or whether? Just remember: **"In cold weather, you wear a sweater."**

Split Infinitives

An infinitive is the basic "to" form of a verb, like "to dance" or "to write." It's incorrect to split infinites.

Splitting infinitives is when you put a word between the "to" and the verb.

Keep in mind the opening line of Star Trek—"To boldly go where no man has gone before"—to remember. The line was mocked by Douglas Adams, who quipped, "To boldly split infinitives that no man had split before."

☐How to Use Commas, Quotation Marks and Semicolons

Creating clean, mostly error-free content is important to freelance writers. Copy full of errors look unprofessional and can really turn off potential customers. You don't want to be lumped in with noobs! Edit!

Emails, blogs and social media encourage speed over accuracy, lulling many into the feeling that close is good enough. If you plan on being a successful freelance writer, though, almost *isn't* good enough. Here are some tips to help you get closer to perfection.

When to Use Commas

Get it right... or scare people away.

One of the most common problems even more skilled writers run into is how to use commas properly.

A comma is defined as a punctuation mark used to indicate

the separation of ideas or elements or a pause in a sentence.

The biggest misuse of commas is often overuse. When in doubt, use a comma when there is an audible pause when you're saying the sentence out loud.

For example:

Jan, can you write the story, please?

This sentence has definite pauses when said aloud. Proper use of commas also keeps the meaning of a sentence clear.

For example:

Wrong - Jan loves to draw fish and write.

Jan likes to draw fish?

Right - Jan loves to draw, fish and write.

Notice that a comma wasn't used after the word "fish." It has become common to leave off the comma before "and" in a series, especially if you are writing for magazines or websites.

The last use of a comma is with a direct name or title.

For example:

The writer and artist, Jan, is my old friend.

Or

Would you draw me a picture, Jan?

Or

Jan Lang, Ph.D., is the author of some impressive articles.

How to Mix Quotation Marks and Punctuation

Using punctuation with quotation marks isn't the mystery some think it is. In fact, there are only two major rules to remember:

Always use punctuation inside the quotation marks.

For example:

"The article is finished. It only took a week to do."

And

Jan said, "It only took a week."

Also, always use a comma before or after a quote is introduced.

For example:

Jan said, "The article is finished."

And

"The article is finished," cried Jan.

"Said" in the first sentence tells you that a quote is coming so it is followed by a comma.

In the second sentence, "cried Jan" tells you who just made the quote. In this case, there is a comma before "cried." Remember, the punctuation is always found inside the quotation marks.

When to Use a Semicolon

Semicolons are an unloved punctuation, mostly because it is misunderstood. If used correctly, though, semicolons are an easy way to spice up a writer's prose, or at least show an editor that the writer is competent.

The rule to follow is: If there are two sentences that are complete thoughts and don't have a conjunction, you can use a semicolon to join them.

For example:

Jan's article is interesting; it is full of great quotes.

Sure, you could put a period between these two statements, but it sounds so much better with a semicolon. Basically, a semicolon shows a close relationship between two sentences and a pause just a little shorter than a period, but longer than a comma.

Now that your copy is treated with respect, romance will be on the way. Your customers will undoubtedly fall in love with the work and you can ride off into the sunset with a check in-hand.

Get Rid of the Junk

There are a few clean-up tips you need to know to make your paragraphs easier to read and more interesting.

First, get rid of "that" whenever you can. If your sentence reads fine without it, toss it.

Next, declare war on "very." Very is a perfectly fine word, but it's boring. The word "very" is almost always unnecessary in your writing.

Mark Twain once said, "Substitute "damn" every time you're inclined to write very. Your editor will delete it and the writing will be just as it should."

Don't wait for the editor!

Here's some ways to mix things up. Change:

- "Very happy" to "jubilant" or "ecstatic"
- "Very eager" to "keen" or "excited"
- "Very painful" to "excruciating" or "agonizing"
- "Very weak" to "feeble" or "frail"
- "Very dry" to "parched" or "dehydrated"
- "Very poor" to "destitute" or "impoverished"
- "Very valuable" to "precious" or "prized"
- "Very neat" to "immaculate" or "tidy"
- "Very bright" to "dazzling" or "blinding"
- "Very hungry" to "starving" or "famished"
- "Very beautiful" to "exquisite" or "stunning"
- "Very strange" to "bizarre" or "unique"
- "Very serious" to "grave" or "solemn"
- "Very sleepy" to "exhausted" or "fatigued"

Chapter 2: How to Make Your Writing Sound Formal or Informal

When you're taking jobs from clients, you'll notice that they will often ask for a "formal" or "casual" tone in your writing style. You need to have a good handle on what these styles are to please your clients. Here's how to make your writing fit with each one.

Formal Style

When you see "formal" think business. It's basically how someone would speak to their CEO or upper management. There's typically:

- No jokes
- No contractions like don't, won't, can't, haven't
- Industry terms
- Third-person point-of-view only (don't use you, I, we, our)

Here's an example of formal writing:

Blog Post: Strategies for Increasing Revenue in a Value-based Healthcare System

Combine Old Techniques with the New

The first step to creating a new revenue cycle that works with a value-based system is to combine the old with the new. The old methods of diagnosis and testing must be combined with new methods that provide a more holistic approach. This method will focus not just on a current ailment, but the patient's entire health and wellbeing as a whole. This for hospitals, this can include:

- Providing better communication techniques

- Incorporating better methods for reducing new infection during hospital stays and outpatient procedures

- Reviewing and organizing data to get a clear view of the patient's overall health before making a diagnosis in the ER

- Encouraging patients to participate in their care by enabling them to track their medical histories and other

personal items easily through the
hospital's website

Target New Demographics

To increase revenue, hospitals must create
programs that will target patients who qualify
for economic programs and are eligible for new
funding sources in line with changes made by
the Affordable Care Act (ACA) for increased
revenue sustainability to compete with other
hospitals in their area. Due to the ACA,
Medicaid has been expanded to include an
increased number of low-income adults. Some
segments that are quickly growing are Dual
Eligible and Hierarchical Condition Categories.

Preparing Patient Financial Service to Properly Handle New Patients

As part of increasing the patient experience, a
provider's patient financial service must be
able to help patients understand health
insurance rules, copays, how networks function
and plan options with patience and
understanding. They also need to learn ways to
guide the patient through the online Medicaid
enrollment process and, if they are in eligible
states, must learn the new guidelines for

determining financial assistance through the ACA to better insure enhanced revenue cycle.

Casual Style

Casual, friendly or informal style is basically how you'd talk to a friend. You would use second person or sometimes first person, and you would use slang, metaphors, jokes and contractions.

Just how casual you can be depends on the website. For example, if you were writing for the New York Times style section, your level of casualness would be a little more laced up than if you were writing for BuzzFeed.

Here's an example of a post written in a casual style:

Blog Post: Why Syndication May be Your Best Content Solution

I recently did a poll of 129 business professionals on what their biggest problems were when it came to posting content to their website. A majority of those polled said that they didn't have time to post or that they couldn't find or write quality content that was fresh and/or innovative.

The results didn't surprise me.

Over the past 16 years I have heard these complaints time and time again. Business owners know that the key to getting more traffic to their site, and more customers, is posting great content search engines and visitors love. It's not an easy task to do when you are running a business, though.

There're usually two solutions.

One, the business owner can hire someone, like me, to create and post content on their site. Two, they can sign up at a syndication site to get pre-made content for their site. Today, I'm going to talk a little bit about syndication for those times when you can't hire someone like me.

You Get Fresh, Relevant Website Content

One of the benefits of getting content from a syndication service is that the content is always fresh and relevant to your industry. One of the biggest complaints from the business owners I polled was that they can never come up with new ideas for articles and blog posts. All they can think of was the same old, tired ideas that their competitors have already covered.

With syndication, you get to pick from the latest articles to hit the web. Since it's unlikely that your competitor uses syndication, you will have the edge.

You Get Quality Content

Chances are, you probably aren't a writer or editor, so writing content yourself is out of the question, at least most of the time. Syndicated articles and blog posts come from the top digital publishers on the web. That means you are getting access to the best writers without the need to hire them. The content has also passed through the hands of some of the best editors on the web, which means the content will look professional, read well and won't contain embarrassing spelling or grammar mistakes.

Get More Traffic

Now, I know what you're thinking. "Doesn't Google penalize sites that have duplicate content?" Yes, they do, but it is important to understand what Google considers duplicate content. The duplication rule only applies if you are posting the same article over and over again on one site (an early black hat SEO tactic). This rule doesn't pertain to an article posted on two *different* sites. So, no, you won't get penalized for using syndicated content that has already been published on another site.

Need proof? Ideal Media found that sites using their syndication service had an 83% increase in traffic. That doesn't sound like those sites are being penalized to me.

So, if you need fresh content, but don't want to create it yourself or hire others to do it for you, consider syndicated content. It could be just what your site needs to rise above your competitors.

Chapter 3: Everything Writers Need to Know About SEO

YOU'VE PROBABLY SEEN JOB ADS LOOKING FOR WRITERS THAT KNOW SEO. IF YOU DON'T KNOW WHAT THOSE THREE LETTERS MEAN, DON'T WORRY. I'M HERE TO HELP!

SEO is an abbreviation for search engine optimization, which, in a nutshell, means anything that helps a search engine find an article and rank it on the first page of search results. Go to Google and search for your favorite topic. See the first result? That article has excellent SEO.

So, how do you get these magical results? Well, only so much of it is in the hands of the writer. A lot of SEO has to do with the website's reputation. I'm going to cover what you, as a writer, needs to know about it to make your articles rank.

Research Keywords

The first thing you do before you write an article is to research. Now, as an expert on your niche, you should have a pretty good idea about what people want to read. There's more to it than that, though. Keywords are a big way search engines know what your article is about and how to rank it in search.

To research keywords, go to *Google Keyword Planner* > **Tools** > **Get Search Volume Data and Trends**. Then, type in a word or phrase that describes what you want to write about and click, **Get Search Volume**.

A list of keywords will pop up. Look for keywords and phrases that have 10 to 100 thousand monthly searches. This means that people are actively typing these keywords into Google each month looking for articles on the topic. And in turn, Google actively searches for articles that provides information on these topics.

So, your articles should have keywords here and there throughout. Most of the time, keywords will naturally pop up in your writing. You don't really need to think about it too hard.

Just be sure that:

- You have a keyword in the title of the article or post and that it is close to the beginning
- There is a keyword in the name of the image files you use and in the captions
- Keywords are in the headings
- There is a least one keyword in the first or second sentence of the post

DO NOT litter your article or post with keywords, though. Other than the areas I've highlighted, let them come naturally. If you spam an article with the same words over and over you'll get a penalty, which will make your post rank *lower* in searches.

SEO-Friendly Headlines

Now you know that your posts should have keywords in the headings, but there is one more thing you should know. All of your headings should have H2 or H3 tags in the code.

Search engines look at your heading to figure out what your article is about. These tags help search engines know where your headings are.

Don't freak out!

You don't need to know coding. Most post editors and word processing software, like Word, have heading options.

Just highlight your heading, tap on the H2 or H3 heading option and you're golden. The tag will be automatically added to the code.

Add Media

Search engines love when you use more than just text in your website content. Plus, media makes your content much more appealing to visitors, which is even more important. You don't want people to come to your posts, see nothing but boring text and click away!

The rule is to add at least two images to your post for good ranking, but the more the merrier. Some media you can add to a post are:

- Embedded videos
- Gifs
- Image galleries
- Audio recordings
- Videos of yourself explaining a concept
- Infographics
- Memes
- Surveys
- Maps

Think creating multimedia content takes too much time? Don't worry. There are plenty of websites out there that help you make your own GIFs, maps, charts, memes and more for free, in just a few minutes. There are also plenty of sites that let you use their multimedia content in your articles.

Try out a couple of these free tools. You'll be adding some snap to your content in no time.

1. PABLO

Have you ever lusted after those sites that have beautiful article images overlaid with pretty quotes or the titles of their articles? Well lust no more. Pablo by Buffer provides you with the beautiful stock images, the fonts and the layering capability. All you need to do is come up with the text.

2. BE FUNKY

I love *Be Funky*. You can use their tools to make your photos totally retro, in a good way. Groovy! They also have stock photos you can use for free.

3. PIC MONKEY

Pic Monkey is one of the most popular free photo editing software sites out there, and for good reason. Not only does it give you the capability to edit photos, you can also use it to create far out photo projects with overlays, frames, textures and more.

4. GIMP

When you need a huge amount of editing tools, but like a zero on the price tag, consider downloading *GIMP*. Think of GIMP as Photoshop's ugly twin. They both have tons of features, but GIMP is a little clunkier to use. Hey, the price is right, though!

5. MEME GENERATOR

Everyone is mad for memes and the Meme Generator makes creating your own simple and quick. Just browse through premade memes, add your own text, download them, and you're in business. Or, you can start from scratch with your own photo. Just upload your photo, fill in the text fields and boom! You've made your own meme.

6. EASEL.LY

Easel.ly is easily the most awesome visual tool I use. (See what I did there?) It gives you everything you need to create stunning infographics and simple drag-and-drop tools. I use it constantly for myself and my customers.

The best part? Easel.ly creates code so that you can embed your infographic on websites.

The free version has a lot of great visuals to start with, but if you want to go pro, I recommend upgrading.

7. GIPHY

Sometimes you just need a snappy gif to make your blog post or social media post just a little more special. Never fear, Giphy is here to supply you will all the gifs your heart could possibly desire, for free.

8. THREE GRAPHS

Need a chart to illustrate some stats? *Three Graphs* is the site to hit up. You can create a variety of different types of charts, choose your chart's colors and more.

9. SIEGE MEDIA EMBEDDED CODE GENERATOR

How many times have you created an awesome visual and then wanted to allow people to share it, but remembered you don't know a thing about creating embedded code? I've been there! The solution is using *Siege Media Embedded Code Generator*. No skill required!

10. MAPBOX

Maps are a cool visual that's not utilized as often as it should be. *MapBox* makes creating your own maps easy and, dare I say it, fun. Just input your data and you're map comes out like you hired Magellan.

Here's a quick list of my 20 favorites and what they do for easy reference:

1. *Giphy for GIFs*

2. *Creative Commons* for Creative Common photos

3. *YouTube* for embeddable videos

4. *Easel.ly* for infographics

5. *Meme Generator*

6. *Pablo for quotes*

7. *PhotoPin* for Creative Commons photos

8. *DaFont* for fonts

9. *Office Sway* for presentations

10. *Pond5* for historic media files

11. *Survey Monkey* for surveys

12. *NVD3* for charts

13. *Mapbox* for maps

14. *OpenClipArt* for clip art

15. *GetEmojis* for emojis

16. *Pexels* for modern, clean photos

17. *PhotoPin* finds Creative Commons photos

18. *MapBox* for maps

19. *Microsoft Sway* online visual creator for newsletters and more

20. *Pexel Videos* for free stock videos

Quality Links Make SEO So Much Better

Finally, you need to add quality links in your articles. Link to reputable sites throughout your articles. Some reputable websites that search engines love are:

- Government sites like the FDA, National Library of Health, or the CDC

- Groups like the World Health Organization, American Dental Association or the American Cancer Society

- Science and health journals and magazines like JAMA and Scientific American

- Trusted health sites like the Mayo Clinic

- University websites

Search engines like it when the link is embedded in words, not just a typed-out address.

Here is an example:

Bad- The site https://moz.com/beginners-guide-to-seo has some good tips for search engine optimization.

Good- The *Moz site* has some good tips for search engine optimization.

Just highlight the words and click on the link tool in the post editor or word processing software to embed your link.

Consider Length

The length of your post or article makes a difference, too. Search engines seem to prefer posts that are 400 words or more. The longer, the better, though. Once again, search engines are looking for value.

If you have a post that is a gallery of images and very little words, don't worry. If there is a lot of media, it seems to cancel out the word count requirement.

Long Content = Good Content, Most of the Time

There've been quite a few studies that discovered Google loves long form content. Long-form is any article or blog post that ranges from 700 words to 2000 words. Long articles are beloved by Google and the population at large because they give in-depth, nitty-gritty, wonderful details about a subject that people want. They aren't just a generic overview that most short article offer.

For example, I do a lot of writing for Live Science. A typical reference article for the site is broken down into sections that will cover every angle of the subject. Take this article on Earth Day that I wrote.

Earth Day: Facts & History

by Alina Bradford, Live Science Contributor | April 21, 2015 05:03pm ET

Earth Day is an annual event created to celebrate the planet's environment and raise public awareness about pollution. The day, marked on April 22, is observed worldwide with rallies, conferences, outdoor activities and service projects.

This composite image uses a number of swaths of the Earth's surface taken on January 4, 2012. Credit: NASA/NOAA/GSFC/Suomi NPP/VIIRS/Norman Kuring

View full size image

Started as a grassroots movement, Earth Day created public support for the creation of the Environmental Protection Agency (EPA) and contributed to the passage of the Clean Air Act, the Water Quality Improvement Act, the Endangered Species Act and several other environmental laws. The idea for Earth Day was proposed by then-Sen. Gaylord Nelson of Wisconsin, who died in 2005.

Before I wrote it, I brainstormed all of the things a person might ask about Earth Day, such as what is Earth Day, who started it, how successful it's been, who celebrates it now, etc. Then, I answered those questions in my article. It has been one of my most successful articles with more than 7,000 shares in just a little over 24 hours.

While I agree that long content does get a lot of search engine love and it gives readers what they want most of the time, you shouldn't get stuck on just adding long-form content to your site.

Why? Here are just a few reasons:

• People love variety. Your regular readers are going to get bored if you continually serve up articles that take 10 to 15 minutes to read.

• People love infographics! Sometimes people want an informative infographic they can skim, and search engines tend to rank infographics, too.

• There are times when people are just looking for a simple answer to their question. Don't go too short, though. Google sees pages with less than 200 words as "thin content."

Be a Good Writer, Darn It!

Search engines also rank posts higher if they contain good spelling. This should go without saying, since you're a professional writer and all, but ALWAYS check your spelling.

That's It!

That's basically all writers need to know about SEO. Remember, as long as you're thinking about your reader and providing quality, then most of your worries are taken care of already.

The Saga of Bogus SEO and Optimization Tactics

Now that you know what to do, I want to tell you what *not to do*. In fact, I want to shout it from the rooftops: Most of the SEO and optimization tactics you'll find online are utterly wrong!

I have talked with many website owners over the years, and it seems like they all have been drinking the same content Kool-Aid. You can't blame them for believing horrible optimization tactics. They were just hungry for some search engine love.

It's time to end the madness, though.

Cutts Says Cut It Out with Article Directories

First, don't use article directories to build links. Oh, I've known so many people that have wandered into this trap...and then Google gave them the website smack down. Finally, Matt Cutts (official leader of everything Google SEO) of Google confirmed what I had always suspected a few years ago. Article directories are slimy, spammy places that gets your articles knocked down in the search engine abyss.

Keywords Aren't as Important as Some People Think

Keywords were once the best way to draw search engine attention. That was a long time ago.

Search engines are smart enough that they can figure out what your content is about without a liberal smattering of keywords. Just add great content to your article and add keywords like I told you to earlier and things will be rosy. Trust me.

Moral of the Story?

Make that blog or article or webpage shine! And if your client asks for bad SEO tactics, firmly tell them that you know what you're doing.

Chapter 4: How to Create Quality Content

Now that you've got some of the basics down, let's dive into how to put an article or post together.

I've been around the block (over and over again) for two decades, so I know what content ranks and what content typically gets drowned out by everything else on the internet. I also know what readers love. Let me clear up some misconceptions and clue you into what's up with quality content.

Build Your Quality with Layering

Rand over at Moz says that to rise to the top, you need content that's 10x better than everyone else's. I wouldn't go that far, but you do need to offer up content that no one else is serving.

Think about your favorite restaurant. You go there because it offers something its competitors don't, like better atmosphere, juicer burgers, tastier pasta or a finer selection of wine. It wouldn't be your favorite if it didn't stand out. Website content is the same. People, and search engines, love content that feeds their needs in a way that others can't.

To create content that stands out, you need a process that I call "content layering."

1.You start with a layer of beefy content. Pepper the text with helpful links, facts and data. Salt it with *Click to Tweet* quotes to make sharing easy.

2.Chop up some long text and turn it into a bulleted or numbered list for easy reading.

3.Slather on a layer of images rich with colors and interesting subject matter that's relevant to the text.

4.Finally, slap on a layer of audio or video content that will make visitors linger and savor your message.

The end result is a site post sandwich that satisfies and excites your visitors and search engine bots.

Mmm, mmm, good!

Create Headlines that Catch Attention

Your article or blog post's headline is the first thing a reader sees. It needs to convey what the content is about and make the person want to read it.

Cute headlines are fun, but if they don't really give your reader a clear idea about what they're going to read, you've failed. They are going to click away.

Here are some tips for coming up with really solid headlines:

1. Answer your readers question. A simple "How to Do XYZ" is often gold.
2. Avoid using click-bait. Titles that scream controversy, offer incredible guarantees or apply similar cheap ploys, can serve a purpose, but only for a moment. If you do end up using click-bait headlines, you need to make sure the body of your copy backs it up in a big way.
3. Grab the readers attention by revealing a shocking fact in your piece. "Your Sink is Filthier than Your Toilet" is a good example. Just make sure the title is true. No clickbait!
4. Use numbers. For some reason, titles with numbers are big hits. For example, my article "20 Unexpected Ways to Use Dryer Sheets" for CNET has garnered millions of views.
5. Add urgency. Make your readers feel like this is information they need right now. For example: "Do These 10 Things Right Now to Increase Your Income" or "Don't Miss Out on These 5 Activities to Do

This Weekend" or "This Writing Mistake is Costing You Clients."

6. Tell your readers they are doing something wrong. For example, "You're Writing Your Headlines All Wrong" could be a good attention grabber. Make sure you follow up with how to fix the problem in the piece, or you just may make your readers mad.

7. Add a little humor. "Annoying 2000s Tech We Kinda Miss" is a title example from one of my articles on No-FluffWriter.com.

8. Keep your titles to 11 words or less. Long headlines are confusing.

9. Put data in your headline. "50 Percent of Writers Don't Have XYZ" is an example of a data driven headline.

10. Use words that show exactly what the format of the article encompasses, like **how to, tips, lessons, guide, ideas, facts, strategies, secrets, gallery, collection, etc.**

11. Use unusual words. Fun use of words get attention and let the reader know this article isn't going to be boring. So, break out that thesaurus. Some of my favorites include awesomesauce, noob, heck, bountiful, heckling, gluttonous, baneful, wee, and assimilate.

12. Use emotion. Add a little emotion to your headline with words like **surprising, funny, shocking, maddening, stunning and helpful.**
13. Try to include **who, what, when, where and how** whenever you can.

Here are some examples from my articles:

By **ALINA BRADFORD** CNET December 21, 2015, 3 56 PM

True or false? Ridiculous microwave myths you can stop believing

21 Tools For Classy Ladies Who Like To Code

We ain't afraid of no Python.

by **mtv news staff** 8m ago

By Alina Bradford

Even though women make up around half of the workforce, they only occupy a little less than 25 percent of science, technology, engineering and math (STEM) jobs. This statistic doesn't mean that the guys are better at STEM jobs, it just means that more

Angie's list

Join Now | How it Works | Sign In | 1-888-888-LIST (5478)

Quick Tour | FAQ | In the Press | Articles | The Big Deal | Business Owners

Home :

Be cautious of online travel planners

Using a travel agent

Several travel agents on Angie's List share the benefits of using this service as well as the pitfalls of planning a trip without a professional agent.

A travel agent prevents disaster vacations

Mistakes a travel agent can prevent

Be cautious of online travel planners

Travel agents consider the kids

Date Published: Oct 02 2012
By Alina Bradford, Angie's List Contributor

The advertisements for websites online and on television claim to make trip planning easy and affordable, but they're not necessarily better than working through a travel agent. Russell J Vara, a Charlotte travel agent at Maestro Travel, offers this opposing view.

By using an online company to plan your trip, you aren't saving as much as you think you are, Russell contends. Online mega sites like Priceline, Orbitz and Expedia have gigantic advertising budgets to convince the consumer that they're getting a substantially better deal by booking all their arrangements themselves -- but their prices are the same as what any travel agency can get you.

Local Offers

Paris, TX (Change)

$49 for Remote Computer Support

My Remote Repair

$129 for a Comprehensive Background Check

CIB Secure Solutions

$49.95 Criminal Records Check

CIB Secure Solutions

---

msn money

Today | Markets | Investing | Personal Finance | Real Estate | Careers | Small Business | Live Coverage | My Watchlist | Mortgages | Credit Cards | Brokers Center | Tools

AS YOU MAY LIKE

5 things to do with your old phone (other than sell it)

© Provided by CNET

If you love having the latest phone, then you probably have a couple of perfectly good phones sitting in a desk drawer or in a closet. They aren't really worth enough to sell, but they still work, so throwing them away isn't an option, either.

It's time to give those cast-offs a new purpose. Here are five ideas to take your old phone from junk drawer fodder to productive member of your household.

QUOTES IN THIS ARTICLE

Turn it into a security camera

If the camera is still good on your old phone, turning it into a security camera is an option. With it, you can keep an eye on your back door, use it as a baby monitor or spy on your pets.

Taylor Martian has a great tutorial on how to turn your old phone into a home security camera so you can watch them anywhere.

Donate it to science (sort of)

Even if you don't want to use your old phone, someone else might. There are a couple apps...

UPS Driver Who Spotted 'Call 911' Scrawled on Package Helps Save Captive Woman

11 REASONS POLAROID IS
MAKING A COMEBACK

TIME TO MAKE IT SNAPPY.

 MTV NEWS STAFF
09/11/2015

By Alina Bradford

When we heard that Polaroid is coming out with a
digital camera that prints photos, we have to admit, we
got a little giddy. Any kid born in the '80s or '90s kinda

 BEST PRODUCTS   REVIEWS   NEWS   VIDEO   HOW TO   SMART HOME   CARS   DEALS   DOWNLOAD   Q

SMART HOME

What do those clothing label symbols
actually mean?

Hint: Pay attention to those symbols on the clothing label.

BY ALINA BRADFORD | MARCH 18, 2016 8:20 PM PDT

Blog Home / Content Marketing / Aline Bradford / 3 Publishers Rocking Sponsored Content

3 Publishers Rocking Sponsored Content

NewCo Shift

LATEST STORIES

Facebook Pivots to Privacy. Why?
March 12, 2019

The Internet Must Change. To Get There, Start With the Data.
January 28, 2019

Predictions for 2019: Data, Tech, Media, Climate, Markets and... Cannabis...
January 2, 2019

One Year Ago: How Our Predictions Fared

Avert Disaster by Backing Up Your Salesforce Data

By alina-bradford

Get Shift Done: Tips and Tricks

Sites go down. Employees make mistakes. Your cat sits on the computer. That's why you need to make sure your important Salesforce data is backed up...just in case.

Add a Dek

A dek is a little line below the headline that gives readers a little more information about what they're about to read. Most websites use deks, written out in sentence form.

To write a successful dek, remember to add to the title, add information, be creative, but be a little bit of a tease, too. Boring deks can drive your readers away.

Here's some examples of decent deks:

Title: You're Thinking too Much About Keywords

Dek: If you're doing this with your keywords you may be making the Google gods angry.

Title: How to Use Deks in an Article

Dek: They're more important than you may think.

Title: You Aren't Doing Your Article Updates Correctly

Dek: Miss these few steps and you'll probably lose your reader.

Avoid Fluffy Content: It's Bad Customer Service

I'm called the No-Fluff Writer for a reason. I preach getting to the heart of the topic right away. Make sure you follow the No-Fluff ways. Don't put fluff in your articles!

What is fluff? Fluff is content that really isn't saying anything helpful. It's basically used to puff up the word count to appease the *SEO Google gods*, or a *demanding client*. Are you giving your clients and readers bad customer service by creating content that doesn't have enough meat?

Think about it while I tell you a little story.

Fluff and Angry Customers

Facebook one day and I saw a post by a popular women's magazine. I liked the title and preview linked in the post, so I clicked and read the article. IT. WAS. BAD.

The article was supposed to be about laundry secrets you just must learn ASAP. The article, though, gave washed up (no pun intended), old advice that anyone within their target audience would already know. A few old tips and done. Nothing *meaty and useful to the reader*.

I was curious to see what others thought of the article, so I clicked back to Facebook and looked at the comments on the post. Almost every single comment was about how basic the article was and how the title was very misleading.

Over the next week or so, I started checking the comments on other articles. The articles that I felt didn't live up to their title or gave simple information that most people already know had so many negative comments. What really shocked me was the multiple offenders. These publications continually drew in readers with flashy titles, then served up mediocre articles that left their readers yawning, confused, or even worse, angry.

Don't make your customers mad with crappy content.

Angry readers matter, my friends. Many of those ticked-off readers that I came across voted with their clicks. In the comments, they stated that they were unfollowing the website and/or canceling their subscriptions.

You know it didn't stop there, right? Those angry people probably told their friends, which probably lead to more bad feelings towards the website and the brand.

How to Stop the Fluff

Articles or blog posts aren't just a great way to bring in views to your site or your client's site.

They are, in a way, a customer service. Sure, you aren't talking directly to potential customers to complete or help with a transaction, but you *are* talking to your customers. You're providing a service with your content.

If you don't spend time crafting a great piece that will be interesting to your readers and delivers on the promise made in the title, then you're giving them poor customer service.

I don't need to tell you that poor customer service makes you lose customers. You know that already.

Give customers what they want: Great content!

Remember that content sandwich from earlier? Here's the elements of a meaty article:

- Research in the form of quotes or data

- Tips that are different from the million other articles on the web on the same topic

- A personal story to illustrate a point

- Testimonials

- Media like gifs, photos, graphs and videos

There is no reason for posting fluff. Just don't do it. Give your customers what they want.

Watch Out for Fluffy Headlines, Too

Many websites draw in visitors from social media sites with sensational headlines, but then fail to deliver in the content.

This is called click-baiting and it results in loss of trust from your visitors. They bounce before clicking on anything else on your site. This, in turn, impacts your conversion rates.

You don't need to have a sensationalist headline to let your readers down, though. Any content that doesn't answer the specific question that the headline promises is poor content.

Chapter 5: Proofreading Techniques

We've been over grammar and spelling in a previous chapter, but I want to talk about the best methods of catching those mistakes in this chapter. Here are a few ways to spot typos before they make it you're your editor, audience or client.

Use Google Translate to Proofread Your Writing (Seriously!)

They say one of the best ways to find errors in your blog posts, book or articles is to read the sentences out loud. An even better method is to have someone else read your piece out loud. This can be difficult if you're a typical writer, alone in your home office.

No problem. A bot can help.

You can use Google Translate as you're editing co-worker. Best of all, it's free.

Just go to the tool at https://translate.google.com. Then, copy and paste your text into the box on the left. Finally, click the sound button to hear your work read aloud.

Read Back-to-Front

Another way to catch typos is to read your paragraphs backwards. I know this doesn't make any sense. How can you catch errors if you're not reading the sentences the way they are intended, right? Trust me. It works.

Read No Less than Three Times

I've made a rule to always check over my work three times before submitting. The times I haven't followed my rule? Yep, there were problems.

Take a Timeout

Before you look over your work one last time, take a breather. Let it marinate as long as you can, then come back. You'll look at the piece with fresh eyes and will notice things you missed before.

You'll Make Mistakes

Oh, writer my friend, you *will* make mistakes. Even with all of the editing and trying and revising you do, you'll put "your" when you mean "you're" or "were" when you mean "where."

When you do, the world will be sure to point it out and try to make you feel like less of a writer. Don't let it bring you down. Everyone, even seasoned professionals, make mistakes.

I mean, look at Christopher Columbus. He went to a whole different continent than intended and named the indigenous people Indians, even though they looked nothing like Indians. Huge screwup on a historical level!

I myself make typos a lot more often than I'd like to admit. Even though this book has been edited probably several dozen times by the time you read it, you'll undoubtedly still find something that isn't perfect.

That's true of most books. Even ones produced my major publishers. (Don't believe me? Go read a book on The New York Times Best Seller list.)

A while back I corrected a typo in an Instagram post and *still* used the wrong spelling. People were quick to let me know about it.

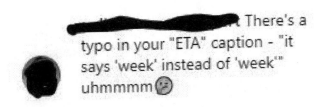

There's a typo in your "ETA" caption - "it says 'week' instead of 'week'" uhmmmm 😕

Mistakes don't make you a bad writer. As long as you make sure that you make as few errors as possible and work hard to make your writing interesting and informative, you'll end up being very successful.

Don't let the fear of errors keep you from writing!

Chapter 6: Speedy Writing Tips for Beginners

Like I've said, I've been in the game of content marketing for, well, a bunch of years. One thing that I've learned well is how to write a blog post and write it quickly. Hey, when you're getting paid by the post, you learn how to be fast!

So, I thought I'd share with my readers my tips for going from an idea to a published post in less than 60 minutes. Got those timers ready? Get ready. Get set. Go!

Reference at Your Fingertips

There are many sites made specifically to aid writers on their quest for information, resources, and education. Below are some of the best to help you save time and get writing.

Everyone knows that you need a good dictionary, thesaurus and encyclopedia, but thumbing through these can waste huge masses of time. Besides, why buy these reference books when you can easily access them on the web? This saves time and money!

Here are a few you should bookmark in your browser:

- Merriam and Webster Online is the best online resources for spelling help and a thesaurus.
- Encyclopedia Britannica has in-depth knowledge almost every topic you can think of when doing research. It also has links to other helpful resources.
- Writer's Market.com is the digital version of this long-time writer's staple offers instant access to thousands of editors and agents just for a few dollars a month. This is a great time saver because it is constantly being updated. No more getting returned query letters because of address changes or business mergers.

Speedy Research

Doing research is one of the biggest time eaters there is for writers. Going to the library can take up a whole day. And typing random terms into search engines can be just as time consuming.

Finding several surefire research sites is the best way to maximize writing time. The key is to stay focused on your topic.

Say you are looking for information on the best places to go salmon fishing. You find several great articles on salmon fishing, but a few popups about salmon recipes. Even if you are tempted, don't stray over to other topics that may pique you interest. Stay focused! It saves precious time that you need to write your story.

Need really detailed information like statistics or government documents for your story? Don't schlep to your local government agency.

Turn to sites like:

- Use Fedstats and USA.gov for demographic information.
- Go to the Centers for Disease Control and Prevention (CDC) website for information and statistics about diseases
- Use Profnet to find experts for quotes.
- Head over to the Mayo Clinic Online for facts about almost any illness you can think of.
- Search the World Health Organization website for world-wide information about illnesses, pandemics, epidemics and more.
- Go to the US Food and Drug Administration (FDA) website for facts about drug testing, current treatments on the market, food safety and more.
- Use the World Bank Open Data site for statistics on countries.

There are more sites listed in the Appendix.

Easy Steps to Writing a Blog Post in Just Minutes

HERE IS YOUR STEP-BY-STEP GUIDE TO WRITING BLOG POSTS FASTER AND BETTER THAN EVER BEFORE.

Figure Out Your Topic

Don't know what to write? Take a look at what others in your field are writing about to brainstorm some ideas using BuzzSumo. Here is a more traditional way to brainstorm, too.

Time: 5 to 10 minutes

Do Your Research

You've got a fantastic idea, but don't start typing yet. First, plug the topic into *Google's Keyword Planner* to decide which keywords will be best for your post. Don't get too caught up in picking, just choose a couple that have low or medium competition but have high monthly search (over 20,000 searches are ideal).

Time: 5 minutes

Summarize Your Content

To make the writing process as fast as possible, summarize the different parts of your post you want to talk about and then use them as your H2 headers.

Time: 5 minutes

Sometimes I look like this when I'm writing a blog post.

Fill in the Blanks

Now that you have your headers, fill in the blanks until you talk about everything you wanted to cover in the post.

Time: 15 to 20 minutes

Finish Up

Now, write the intro, the closing paragraph and the call to action. Once you have those wrapped up, don't forget to write a meta description.

Time: 10 to 15 minutes

Add Some Media

Add some flash (and some search engine love) to your post by adding some media. Search for free content or create your own using. Remember these from earlier?

- Giphy for gifs
- Meme Generator
- Pablo for quotes

- *PhotoPin* for Creative Commons photos
- *Creative Commons* for Creative Common photos
- YouTube for embeddable videos
- *NVD3* for charts
- *Mapbox* for maps
- *OpenClipArt* for clip art
- *Survey Monkey* for surveys
- *Office Sway* for presentations
- *Pond5* for historic media files
- *GetEmojis* for emojis

Time: 10 minutes

That's all there's to my process. Pretty simple, huh? Trust me, once you get the hang of it, you can crank out blog posts in just 15 to 30 minutes without breaking a sweat!

When Things Get Hard, Use an Article Quality Checklist

Stupid mistakes are my nemesis when my mind is distracted. The best thing to do is to try your best, but also fall back on a checklist to be sure you didn't miss anything before you submit the work. It's the fast way to catch mistakes.

This checklist will help you create quality articles and blog posts, no matter what type of stress you're facing.

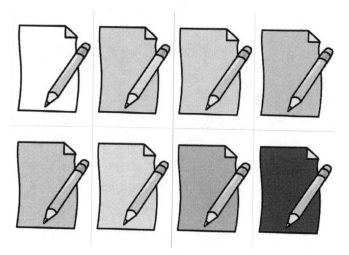

- Does the title make sense?

- Is the title in the right style of capitalization for the publication? For example, are all the words capitalized? Or just this first?

- Does the title have good flow and include keywords?

- Take out the unnecessary "that" words found in your article.

- Check your "it's" and "its" to make sure they are correct.

- Are the headers in H3 or H2, depending on your client's requirements?

- Are there enough photos?

- Did you meet the word count requirement, if there is one?

- Take a look at all of the "an" and "a" words in your article. If they come before a word with a vowel, remember the it should be "an" not "a."

- Did you link to any sources or cite your sources correctly, depending on the needs of the client?

- Do all your sentences flow well? Remember to mix compound sentences and simple sentences throughout a paragraph to make the rhythm interesting.

- Make sure your paragraphs transition well.

- Are all of the sentences punctuated correctly?

- Cut any repetitions or unneeded words. (Remember, no fluff!)

- Does the overall theme fit the idea of the article, or did you go off track?

- Did you break down complicated steps into numbered lists?

- Did you make a group of items into bulleted lists for easy reading?

- If your article or blog has keywords, did you make sure to use them naturally, so they don't seem awkward?

- Is there a Call to Action or something to lead the reader to another page?

- Did you use first, second or third person throughout?

- Is the article or blog the right tone? Is it too formal or too casual, for example?

- Pretend you've never read this post before and know little about the subject. Is any of it confusing?

- Are there any videos or gifs you can embed to make the post more interesting?

- Did you include easy ways to follow you on social media though call-to-action or follow buttons?

Chapter 7: No-Fluff Guide to Building Your Freelance Business Brand

Your brand is what makes you stand out from the crowd, writers. So, as you build your freelance writing business, you need to focus on what makes you *you* and how you're going to convey that to the masses.

You may be saying, "Wait, Alina, what does this have to do with creating content for my clients?"

Learning branding is not only good for your business, but it can also help you create better content for your clients. When you understand branding, you can help your customer develop their own brand through your articles and blog posts.

This No-Fluff guide will walk you through the process.

What is Branding?

Branding is a huge buzzword right now, but it is so much more than a trend. No matter what you call this type of marketing, companies big and small depend on it to compete in competitive markets.

Branding definition: Making your brand stand out from competitors with marketing that is consistent and recognizable as belonging to only *your* company.

Keeping a consistent message, tone and feel to your marketing makes people remember you and that is a HUGE part of selling. Content on your website plays a big part in this image.

Businesses Are Going About Their Branding Process All Wrong

Life isn't a contest, though. Often, when freelancers start to visualize their brand, they think about all of the other competitors out on the market. They wonder how they can be the best.

Years ago, I tried to write an inspirational quote or a tidbit of knowledge that I've gleaned along the way on the bathroom mirror each night for my girls to see before they head off to school the next morning. One night, I wrote:

<u>There is always going to be someone smarter, prettier, faster, etc. Be the best YOU can be. Life isn't a contest.</u>

I think too many people get caught up in what everybody else is doing and they don't focus enough on what makes their brand special. Notice I said "special" and not "better."

Proving your better than someone else is like trying to prove you love your spouse to someone who doesn't know you. You can show them all the proof in the world, but they still won't be 100% sure.

That's because all humans are just a little suspicious of each other. In the back of our minds we're wondering if that guy really loves his wife or if he's cheating with Ms. Robertson next door.

It's the same with businesses. They say they're the best, but are they just full of hot air?

When people look at your branding, don't make them wonder if you're just full of hot air. Give them a positive feeling and you are off to a great start. Get them to laugh or feel nostalgic or feel at home.

That's what branding is all about. Conveying a feeling right off the bat and threading that feeling through everything that you present to your customer.

Assignment: What's Your Brand?

I'm going to ask you some questions. Answer them as honestly as possible. Let's get started.

Will you be the face of your freelance business? For example, I am the face of my company. In fact, my company name is my own personal name. My company is 100% my voice and no one else's. Another example would be Dave Thomas of Wendy's. The restaurant was named after his daughter and her face was the logo, but he was the one that stared in many of the early commercials. His face, voice and sense of humor were what cemented Wendy's brand.

If you don't want your freelance business to center around you, no problem. We can work with that! You just need to know how you are going to present your business to the world.

- Will you have a logo instead of a professional photo to represent your business?
- Will your business be your name or will you come up with something else to call it?

- What colors will represent your business? Remember, branding needs consistency.

What do you think is special about you? For example, do you have a passion for the environment and want to be seen as a "green" freelancer? Could your former job give you an interesting insight into your niche that you could capitalize on?

Get the Sizzle: 5 Steps for Building Your Brand Identity with Your Website

Building your brand identity starts with your website. Everything you add to your site will affect how visitors will feel about your freelance writing business. Revamping your site to create a more cohesive brand is the best way to boost sales and make customers remember you.

Branding with Colors

Step one is the most visual way to brand your site. Using one or two colors throughout your site, marketing items and packaging creates is more than just making things matchy-matchy. It gives consumers a visual clue as to who you are.

It has even been proven that colors can influence purchases. So, choose one or two colors that will represent your business, ideally colors already used in your logo.

Branding with Font

Like colors, you need to pick two to three fonts, tops, that will be used on your site. Mimic the font used on your packaging or in your logo for headers or H1 titles. Be sure that your page text is easily readable, though.

Branding with Your Logo

Now, your logo isn't just for the header of your website. Use it throughout. Watermark images with it. Use it on your about page. Use it in the footer. Be sure that you use it throughout your site.

Branding with Images

Have you ever been to a website that uses images that all seem to go together? That theme is their image brand. If you visit my site often, you'll probably notice that I use a lot of GIFs and fun images. I like to keep things light while talking about serious subjects. That's my brand.

You can do it, too. Come up with a theme for your images and be consistent. For example, product images could all have the same background or images could all work together in a common theme such as nature, modernism, zen, etc.

Branding with Content Tone

Once you have the visuals in place, concentrate on the tone of your text. Every article, blog post, content description, etc, should have the same tone. Don't bounce from fun and peppy to straight-laced and staunch. Stay the same. Let consumers know who you are. Build a personality through your text.

6 Ways to Make Your Site Traffic Soar

Now that you have branding down, it's time to get traffic to your website so you can pick up customer. These tips will also help you learn how to draw in traffic for your customers.

Update Your Content

With changes in rules, regulations, laws and the way technology are advancing at an amazing pace, something you wrote on your website 6 months ago could be totally out of date and mislead anyone that reads it. You need to reread all of the past articles and blogs and update any of them that fall into this category. Search engines will see the post as still being relevant and that can help with your SEO rankings.

A good update includes:

- A new title
- New intro paragraph
- Two links to other content on your site in the intro paragraph
- Broken links are fixed
- More media, if you can find some good stuff
- Publish it as a new article, but leave the address the same

Use Ads to Move Up the Rankings

Most times, when you put something into your search engine, the top few results will say 'ad' at the side. This is because businesses have paid to be in one of the top spots.

Getting your own ad can be well worth the money invested because then your page is much more likely to be linked to by viewers, raising your rank.

Make the Most of Social Media

Social media is a must for all businesses. It's a vital way of getting your brand known and an awesome way to send more traffic to your website.

You should post every day, at least, but do not make all your posts promotional. If you do, users will start to scroll past your posts without bothering to read them.

One promotional post out of five is a good rule of thumb. Some people post 20 percent promotional content and 80 percent other content. Your mix will depend on your target audience.

Don't just use memes, photos and text posts, either. Videos are sometimes the best way to attract attention to your brand, and if they contain some humor, they are likely to be shared.

Also, always respond to any comments in a positive manner. This will help to build trust in your business and make you look like a professional. Nobody wants to deal with rudeness.

Be sure to put a link to your site on all your posts to drive traffic. On Instagram, using your website address as a watermark is a good idea.

Email Marketing

Email marketing fell out of favor for a while but now it is back. It is a great way to stay connected with existing customers or to make connections with new ones.

To be effective, each email has to be interesting or solve a problem for your audience, and it should always have a link to your website included.

Run a Contest

Running a contest is a great way to attract new traffic. You just have to make sharing a link to your site one of the rules of entry. Another smart rule is they must enter with their email address so you can add this to your mailing list.

Optimize for Mobile

Around 80 percent of internet use is done on mobile devices. This percentage is likely to grow, I mean, smartphones are little more than handheld computers. So, it makes sense to be sure to optimize your site for mobile devices.

Optimizing means making your site responsive in terms of being easy and attractive to use on a mobile device.

Plus, your site needs to respond quickly to user clicks and swipes on mobile. A page load time of just 7 seconds can increase your bounce rates (people who leave) by over 30%.

Pro tip: You can check your site for free using Google page speed tool, Page Speed Insights.

Make Your Blog More Professional

When it comes to the design of a blog, it should be clean, professional, and mobile-friendly. But, what else?

Let's take a look.

Font

Use an easy-to-read font. Once you have found the one that works for you, you should be use it across all of your content.

Some good fonts are:

- New Times Romans
- Georgia
- Open Sans
- Verdana
- Roboto
- Arial
- Impact

Clutter

Get rid of the clutter. While you might be looking to make your blog your primary source of income, a lot of inline ads, pop-ups and other flashy items are likely to put your reader off. When in doubt put them in the sidebar.

Images

Use full-width images when you can. Beautifully written content filled with emotion or information will go to waste if your images are fixed width and small.

The flow of the material, in pretty much any content, will be much better when you use full-width images. It is much more aesthetically pleasing. Uniformity is beautiful.

Also, a good tip is to break up large blocks of text with your images. This will keep readers interested.

Fold

You need to utilize the space above the fold. If you have a really large header, and then some adverts, you are forcing people to scroll down to read your content. It isn't always a bad thing but think about how often you scroll down on a site. I bet it isn't often. If you don't get a peek at what you need right away, you're clicking away.

Any content above the fold needs to be the hook, you need to tell people WHY they need to read the rest of the post. What does scrolling down give them? Nothing!

Tests

The code for some themes changes, plugins change, and everything updates. If you aren't checking in on the content, you might find that people are having problems you weren't aware of.

When you perform a check use the menu to navigate through the blog, try scrolling down and see at what point your pop-ups arrive. All of this will benefit or inhibit your readers. The user experience is essential.

Chapter 8: Brainstorming Ideas

The worst part of running a writing business is when you don't have any ideas for an article or post. It's that oh s**t moment.

No matter what sort of writer you are, you'll get blocked sometimes. Even JK Rowling suffered terrible writer's block when she was trying to write *Harry Potter and the Chamber of Secrets*. Luckily there are a few things you can do to get yourself through writer's block and back into a creative frame of mind.

Get Away from the Desk

If your writer's block is just a momentary thing and you haven't been suffering for months, the best thing to do is to get up from your desk and go for a walk.

Whether you get a cup of tea and go to sit outside for half an hour, or you strap on your walking boots and get down and dirty with nature for an afternoon, is up to you - but it's important to change your environment.

You could even move your laptop to a different place in the house for a slightly different perspective. I like to sit at my patio table in my yard.

Try Free Writing

Pick up a pen and paper and write for fifteen minutes without stopping, even if your hand starts to cramp up. If you have an obliging friend, ask them to read out words to you for inspiration.

Although a lot of what you write won't be useful in the slightest, chances are there will be a few phrases in there that will be interesting simply because you didn't have a chance to think about them before you wrote them down. Free writing can show you what's really in your head by lowering your inhibitions.

Experience Other Stories

If you're suffering from an ability to structure your writing, why not take in other people's stories? Watch a great season of TV or a movie in a similar genre. For example, if you're writing a gangster novel, watch the likes of The Godfather and The Sopranos.

Do a Throwback

For bloggers, sometimes, to create great content you don't need to create *new* content. One look at your former posts can supply you with a plethora of awesome future posts.

For example, do a roundup of your most popular posts. Go to your site stats and take a look at the posts that got the most views, the most comments or the most shares. Choose the top ten and create a post that links to each other with a brief description of why each post rocks. Better yet, add your favorite line or tip from each post to the description.

Another idea for repurposing old posts is by expanding on them. Do an update or flesh out the old post with new or more complex information.

For example, on one of my sites (I sold the site in 2014) I wrote a post on how to draw people. Then I broke that general information post down into more in-depth posts, such as How to Draw a Child, How to Draw a Nose, How to Draw a Mouth, and a dozen other posts.

Mind Maps

Another way to find ideas, do a brainstorming session with mind maps. Draw a circle on a piece of paper and write the name of the post in the circle.

Now draw some smaller circles around the large one. Fill these circles with topics that stem from the main topic in the main post.

Branch out from these ideas with circles with even more detailed ideas.

Here is an example:

How Website Colors Affect Sales

Why Your Theme Doesn't Work

Hot Wordpress Colors

Worst WordPress Themes

Top 5 WordPress Themes

Wordpress Theme Customizing Options

Brainstorming Example

Best WordPress Themes with Header Options

alinabradford.com

Do a Survey

If you want 100% new ideas for your blog or articles, then mine your readers. Set up a survey (SurveyMonkey is a good app to use) and ask them about what their biggest concerns are. Then, craft posts that answer their questions or concerns. This one tactic can give you a lot of great topics to work with and the best part is your readers will really care about your posts.

Read Books

Another super helpful tactic is reading the posts of other people in your industry. You may find that you have such a strong reaction to something you read that you simply must write a rebuttal.

Here is an example:

Neal Frankle says that going to college can be a waste of time and money. While in some cases I would agree, my own experience has shown me that even half a degree can be worth your while.

One post can even spawn ideas for several others. I took the one post by Neal Frankle and used it to spur ideas for another post for one of my clients.

Read Poetry

One of the great things about poetry is that each one is like a short story - a poem is a representation of a thought on the page instead of a long, labored plot structure. If you're having problems writing and you're feeling jealous of other writers, you could read some poetry from the older Romantic poets like Wordsworth to more recent poets like the spoken word poet Andrea Gibson.

Reading poetry will help you appreciate the beauty and importance of carefully choosing each word and it will help you write sentence by sentence instead of thinking of your article as an enormous task that you will inevitably fail at.

Listen to Music

Crank up your favorite jam and rock out. The burst of feel good chemicals can get your brain working.

If that doesn't work, try listing to a genre that you usually don't like or listen to. The change may be enough to startle your brain into work mode.

Brainstorm by Sleeping

Some of the greatest ideas have come about by sleeping. American author John Steinbeck wrote, "A problem difficult at night is resolved in the morning after the committee of sleep has worked on it."

Many other great minds have felt the same way about the power of sleep. Einstein's theory of relativity supposedly began with a dream about a field full of cows surrounded by an electric fence. The song "Yesterday", drifted to Paul McCartney while he slept in 1964 and The Terminator came to director James Cameron in a dream many years later.

The periodic table came to the Russian chemist Dmitri Mendeleev in his sleep in 1869. "I saw in a dream a table where all the elements fell into place as required," he wrote. "Awakening, I immediately wrote it down on a piece of paper. Only in one place did a correction later seem necessary."

How can you harness the power of sleep?

1. Ask yourself a question before you go to sleep or focus on the problem at hand.
2. Set timers so that you'll wake up throughout the night. Both Salvador Dalí and Thomas Edison would be sure to get woken up just as they drifted off to capture ideas.
3. Keep a notebook beside your bed so you can write any revelations down when you wake up.
4. Practice lucid dreaming. This is a difficult skill of being aware while you're dreaming. There are several good books on the topic.

Focus on a Writing Project Outside Your Comfort Zone

We also tend to get caught doing the same jobs. It makes sense for security purposes, but it can also lead to blockages. If you're writing the same articles from different angles, it's no wonder your ideas have stopped flowing.

If you're struggling, accept it and step away. It may mean losing some money, but it allows you to focus on something else. And, that could be a Godsend.

This could involve anything. You may want to write a story instead of a news piece, or a poem instead of fiction. You may even want to spread your love of words in schools. In this instance, you could start a school magazine and distribute it.

Learn a New Craft

5.

If crafts get your juices flowing, it may be time to put down the pen altogether. Learning a new craft, like knitting, allows you to keep creativity flowing, while also learning something new. Since knitting is a relatively passive craft, it leaves your mind free to come up with new ideas.

Get a New Active Hobby

Being active pumps happy chemicals to your brain. These chemicals can make you more creative, leading to great ideas you never thought of before.

Chapter 9: Take My 30-Day Blog Challenge

Now that you know the basics of web writing, let's practice with this 30-day challenge. It will build your skillset and help you create content that you can show to potential clients.

Let's get started!

DAY 1

Today is all about building the foundation. Start by brain dumping every post idea you can think of into a notebook. There are no stupid ideas, but make sure you stay on topic.

If your site is about bathroom products don't write down post ideas that revolve around gardening, for example. Need help with ideas? Take a look at this brainstorming help.

DAY 2

Now that you have a list of possible post topics, go through and pick out your top eight ideas. That will give you two posts per week for a month.

DAY 3

In your notebook, make a page for each article idea. Write an idea at the top of each page. On the pages write out a few lines about what each post would cover. This is another time to brain dump!

DAY 4

Now is the time to write your first post. Write an introduction, and then write a subheading for every item you want to talk about in the post. This will get your thoughts organized.

Fill in the information in detail and then sum everything up at the end. After your closing paragraph add a CTA (Call to Action.) You can see an example of a CTA at the end of this post.

DAY 5

Now that you have a post, go over it and check for spelling and grammar mistakes. Then, give it a rocking title.

DAY 6

Pick some photos for your post. Make sure you save the photos with keyword-rich terms and give them a title, caption, alt text and description that is also keyword-rich. This will help with your ranking.

Also, the more photos you have, the better, so pick at least two images to accompany your post.

DAY 7

Post that post! You're ready to fly! Use a site like Buffer to set up a schedule for social media links to your new content. You'll want a link to post right away, one in eight hours, one in 24 hours, on in a week and one in a month on Twitter. On other social media sites, post once immediately and then once again in a month or so.

DAY 8

Okay, you've got a great post under your belt. Now what? Start on the next post! Now that you know how, you can start writing your posts at a faster rate. Write the whole post out today!

DAY 9

Great content isn't just about text posts.
Visuals are amazing tools for getting pageviews
and loyal fans.

So, today, take a video of yourself talking about
your brand or a great product you offer. Post it
to YouTube and embed it to create a new post
on your site.

DAY 10

A sample of infographics that can be made over at easel.ly.

Another great visual to add to your site is infographics. You can create your own infographics for free at *easel.ly*. Use one of the blog topic ideas that you didn't use for inspiration for your infographic.

DAY 11

Remember that post you wrote on Day 8? Post that sucker!

DAY 12

Get to work on your next blog post.

DAY 13

A good way to boost your site rank is to check the amount of text on all your posts and pages.

Google considers a page or post with less than 200 words not worth people's time. Write down a list of all the pages that need a boost in content.

DAY 14

Choose two pages from the list you made yesterday and add some content to them.

DAY 15

Post your blog post that you wrote on Day 11.

DAY 16

Write your next blog post.

DAY 17

Dead or broken links can lower your page rank. Use a tool like Broken Link Checker by Janis Elsts to find and fix broken links.

DAY 18

Make another video post. Concentrate on showing your personality while you talk.

DAY 19

Get Day 16's post up on your blog.

DAY 20

Write your next post.

DAY 21

Choose two pages from the list you made on Day 13 and add some content to those pages.

DAY 22

Make it easier for visitors to share your content. Add social media sharing buttons to your site. I personally like Flare. Only link to three different social media sites, though. This gives you better interaction by not overwhelming your readers with choices.

DAY 23

Have a social media Q and A. Invite people on social media to ask you questions for an hour and answer the questions in real time. Be sure

to link to any posts you have that will give a
more in-depth answer.

DAY 24

Post Day 20th's blog post.

DAY 25

Write your next post.

DAY 26

Video post day! Make a post about why you
started your business and how you hope it will
help your customers.

DAY 27

Choose two pages from the list you made on
Day 13 and add some content to those pages.

DAY 28

Get your meta descriptions for your pages and posts in sparkling condition. Make it easy by using a plugin like *Yoast*.

DAY 29

Post Day 25th's blog post.

You made it across the finish line! Good job!

DAY 30

Write your next blog post.

You did it!

Congratulations on finishing a whole month of content creation and clean up! You should be seeing more pageviews, better ranking on search engines and more interaction in the comments section and on social media.

Chapter 10: 50 Writing Tips from the Experts

I'd like to finish this book off with some wisdom. What better place to find wisdom than from experienced writers?

Here are 50 writing insights from some of the world's best.

1. The first draft of everything is shit. —*Ernest Hemingway*

2.Remember: when people tell you something's wrong or doesn't work for them, they are almost always right. When they tell you exactly what they think is wrong and how to fix it, they are almost always wrong. – *Neil Gaiman*

3.Write drunk, edit sober. – *Ernest Hemingway*

4. Interesting verbs are seldom very interesting. – *Jonathan Franzen*

5. The road to hell is paved with adverbs. – *Stephen King*

6. If it sounds like writing, I rewrite it. – **Elmore Leonard**

7. If you don't have time to read, you don't have the time — or the tools — to write. Simple as that. – **Stephen King**

8. Being a writer is a very peculiar sort of a job: it's always you versus a blank sheet of paper (or a blank screen) and quite often the blank piece of paper wins. – **Neil Gaiman**

9. You can only write regularly if you're willing to write badly… Accept bad writing as a way of priming the pump, a warm-up exercise that allows you to write well. – **Jennifer Egan**

10. When you're trying to create a career as a writer, a little delusional thinking goes a long way. –**Michael Lewis**

11. Perfectionism is the voice of the oppressor, the enemy of the people. It will keep you cramped and insane your whole life. –**Anne Lamott**

12. Work on one thing at a time until finished. — *Henry Miller*

13. You have to simply love writing, and you have to remind yourself often that you love it. — *Susan Orlean*

14. Create blog posts that answer the most interesting questions from people you engage with on social media. — *Dave Larson*

15. Understand your audience better than they understand themselves. It takes a lot of upfront research, and often means being a member of

the very tribe you're trying to lead – but it pays off. **– *Brian Clark***

16. Write for yourself first & foremost. Ignore the fact that anyone else will read what you write; just focus on your thoughts, ideas, opinions and figure out how to put those into words. Write it and they will come. **–*Adii Pienaar***

17. Start building your email list from day one. Even if you don't plan on selling anything, having an email list allows you to promote your new content to your audience directly without worrying about search rankings, Facebook EdgeRank, or other online roadblocks in communications. **– *Kristi Hines***

18. Love the readers you already have. A lot of bloggers get quite obsessed with finding new readers – to the point that they ignore the ones they already have. Yes – do try to find new readers but spend time each day showing your current readers that you value them too and you'll find that they will help you grow your blog. – **Darren Rowse**

19. Consistency is one of the most important things that bloggers tend to forget. It's much easier to lose your traffic than it is to build it up, so make sure you consistently blog. – *Neil Patel*

20. Stay true to yourself and your voice. People don't care to follow sites so much as they care to follow people. – *Chris Pirillo*

21. No matter how great your content is, it won't matter unless you *have an amazing headline*. People have a split second to decide if they should click on your post, and your headline will make them decide. The headline is also essential in making it easy and desirable for people to share your post. Keep your headlines SPUB: simple, powerful, useful and bold. – **Dave Kerpen**

22. Biggest lesson I learned in my past year of blogging. Keep it in the 1–2 minutes read-time length. – *Derek Sivers*

23. One thing I always try to keep in mind before publishing a post is would anyone want to "cite" this for any reason? Just like interesting research is great because it leaves you with a fascinating finding or an idea, I like for my posts to be the same. That doesn't mean relying on research, but simply making sure each post has an original lesson or actionable item, making it "citable" on the web. – *Gregory Ciotti*

24. Be efficient, and don't put things off that you could do right now. No more self-sabotage or "next week" lists. Don't over-prepare and never do the things you're preparing for. Just be here, in the now, and be as productive as you can today. Write now, edit later. – *Deborah Stachelski*

25. Remember, your blog is one of your first opportunities to connect with new potential clients. It's often the first impression you make on a new person! You wouldn't want to shake hands with a new potential client with a huge piece of spinach in your teeth and garlic breath and having poorly written content on your website is essentially the same thing (maybe worse). – *Allison Volk*

26. Your path may look completely different than others, and it should. Creating your own unique blog is what you need to do in order to stand out from the others. The world does not need any more duplicates. — *Gabrielle Pfeiffer*

27. Vigorous writing is concise. — *William Strunk Jr.*

28. I try to leave out the parts that people skip. — *Elmore Leonard*

29. As one who writes a lot for the web, I am continually tempted by the low-hanging fruit of trending topics and morning news drivel. Restating the obvious is easy, fun, and very retweetable. But the obvious rarely seems to translate into any sort of real legacy. — *Seth Simonds*

30. The difference between the right word and the almost right word is the difference between lightning and a lightning bug. — *Mark Twain*

31. I use a moleskine to store my thoughts for later. Having thoughts and personal commentary all in one place has the added benefit of serving as a source of inspiration for later times of drought. Think of it as you would catching raindrops in a canteen. You'll be glad for the moisture some day. — *Seth Simonds*

32. Every writer I know has trouble writing. — *Joseph Heller*

33. While having an outline can be incredibly helpful in keeping your thoughts moving and on track, you will actually write more quickly and produce higher-quality writing if you start before you know everything that you want to say. The writing process is creative and interactive, so you will develop ideas and thoughts as you write. — *Christine Zosche*

34. When you sit down to write your tips and tales from the road, ask yourself: what do I want the reader to learn from this? What's the take-away? Then craft a tightly constructed piece that leads, step by step, to that lesson-point. — *Don George*

35. When you write a blog post, you have to create a series of mental images so colorful that your readers could see how a pan sizzles when a patty is put on or even the smell of a recently cooked carrot patty. — *Emily Sidley*

36. Don't think of words when you stop but to see picture better — *Jack Kerouac*

37. Don't get depressed that you're abandoning your artistry, because you're not. On the contrary, you're building a foundation for it. Once you *become adept at freelancing*, you not only have income to use for your dream

project, but — surprise! You've vastly improved your writing skills. And people now identify with you as a professional writer. — *The Write Life*

38. Whichever way you get into freelancing, the absolute key to success is persistence. Chances are you'll get knocked back a fair bit but keeping going is the only way to ensure that you get noticed. — *Laura Kay*

39. Freelancing is probably not for people who lack self-motivation. If you don't go looking for work, spending your days shooting off emails and writing pitches, then it is very unlikely the work will come to you. — *Laura Kay*

40. Stop trying to figure out the one, best, fastest, lowest-cost way to launch your freelance writing career. Stop endlessly fretting over what your most ideal writing niche might be and how you will know which topics will be best for you. Stop worrying that you're not good enough or don't know enough. Instead, take action. — *Carol Tice*

41. If you are just getting started as a freelance writer, your best bet is to begin taking on small projects in order to *build up a portfolio*. Ask your first clients to start attributing articles to your name and ask if you can get an author biography with a picture of yourself on their website. — *Katie Cline*

42. Don't pat yourself on the back in your blog posts, bragging about what you know about your industry. Let your blog visitors find the value themselves in the content you produce. — *William Morrow*

43. Write, write, write, and then write some more. Forget everything else and just write. — *Melissa Donovan*

44. Use the time of a total stranger in such a way that he or she will not feel the time was wasted. — *Kurt Vonnegut*

45. The only rule is work. If you work it will lead to something. It's the people who do all of the work all of the time who eventually catch on to things. — *John Cage*

46. Be your own editor/critic. Sympathetic but merciless! — *Joyce Carol Oates*

47. Don't try to anticipate an ideal reader or any reader. He/she might exist but is reading someone else. — *Joyce Carol Oates*

48. Protect the time and space in which you write. Keep everybody away from it, even the people who are most important to you. — *Zadie Smith*

49. Write for scanners. We live in a busy, distracted world. Don't demand attention; earn it. — *Jeff Goins*

50. Don't take anyone's writing advice too seriously. — *Lev Grossman*

Appendix

Quick List of My 20 Favorite Sites for Free Media

1. *Giphy for GIFs*

2. *Creative Commons* for Creative Common photos

3. *YouTube* for embeddable videos

4. *Easel.ly* for infographics

5. *Meme Generator*

6. *Pablo for quotes*

7. *PhotoPin* for Creative Commons photos

8. *DaFont* for fonts

9. *Office Sway* for presentations

10. *Pond5* for historic media files

11. *Survey Monkey* for surveys

12. *NVD3* for charts

13. *Mapbox* for maps

14. *OpenClipArt* for clip art

15. *GetEmojis* for emojis

16. *Pexels* for modern, clean photos

17. *PhotoPin* finds Creative Commons photos

18. *MapBox* for maps

19. *Microsoft Sway* online visual creator for newsletters and more

20. *Pexel Videos* for free stock videos

Reliable Websites to Use for Free, Credible Research and Citations

To find specific information on these sites google **(topic) : (site name)**. For example, if I were looking for information about lions I would google **lions : National Geographic.**

- Profnet (to find experts for original quotes)
- U S Food and Drug Administration (FDA)
- National Library of Health
- Centers for Disease Control and Prevention (CDC)
- World Health Organization (WHO)
- American Dental Association
- American Cancer Society
- The Journal of the American Medical Association (JAMA)
- Scientific American
- Mayo Clinic Online

- University websites
- Drugs.com
- American Academy of Pediatrics
- National Center for Biotechnology Information
- U.S. National Library of Medicine
- National Institute of Health
- Encyclopedia Britannica Online
- Geological Society of America
- U.S. Geological Survey
- The World Bank Open Data site (for world-wide demographic information)
- Merriam-Webster Dictionary Online
- Oxford Dictionary Online
- National Geographic Online
- ITIS (Animal classification site)
- International Union for Conservation of Nature and Natural Resources
- IUCN Red List of Threatened Species (endangered species list)
- National Science Foundation

- University of Michigan's Museum of Zoology

- Smithsonian National Museum of Natural History

- The Natural History Museum

- American Museum of Natural History

- Public Broadcasting Service (PBS)

- Fedstats and USA.gov (for US demographic information)

Pro tip: Need a specific scientific study for your research, but don't want to pay to access it through a scientific journal? Email the author or university that produced the paper and they will send you a free copy.

Article Quality Checklist

- Does the title make sense?

- Is the title in the right style of capitalization for the publication? For example, are all the words capitalized? Or just this first?

- Does the title have good flow and include keywords?

- Take out the unnecessary "that" words found in your article.

- Check your "it's" and "its" to make sure they are correct.

- Are the headers in H3 or H2, depending on your client's requirements?

- Are there enough photos?

- Did you meet the word count requirement, if there is one?

- Take a look at all of the "an" and "a" words in your article. If they come before a word with a vowel, remember the it should be "an" not "a."

- Did you link to any sources or cite your sources correctly, depending on the needs of the client?

- Do all your sentences flow well? Remember to mix compound sentences and simple sentences throughout a paragraph to make the rhythm interesting.

- Make sure your paragraphs transition well.

- Are all of the sentences punctuated correctly?

- Cut any repetitions or unneeded words. (Remember, no fluff!)

- Does the overall theme fit the idea of the article, or did you go off track?

- Did you break down complicated steps into numbered lists?

- Did you make a group of items into bulleted lists for easy reading?

- If your article or blog has keywords, did you make sure to use them naturally, so they don't seem awkward?

- Is there a Call to Action or something to lead the reader to another page?

- Did you use first, second or third person throughout?

- Is the article or blog the right tone? Is it too formal or too casual, for example?

- Pretend you've never read this post before and know little about the subject. Is any of it confusing?

- Are there any videos or gifs you can embed to make the post more interesting?

- Did you include easy ways to follow you on social media though call-to-action or follow buttons?

30+ Sites that Offer Quick Freelance Writing Gigs

Now that you know how to write content you need to know of some places to look for gigs.

Here are more than 30 to check out.

1. Scripted: This is one of the best paying sites. Short posts are often go for around $50 after the site takes a cut. Some clients offer much more. They also work with big brands like eBay and StubHub.

2. Contently: This site gives writers free, awesome portfolios and often assigns high-paying gigs. One of my gigs there paid $360 per article.

3. DotWriter: You can get gigs on this site and also sell articles that you haven't placed elsewhere.

4. Textbroker: I'm not going to say this site pays really well, but there's lots of work.

5. Study.com: If you have a degree, you can teach classes and make some good money.

6. Article Document: I've heard good things about this site.

7. Blogmutt: This site has a lot of really easy, fast gigs.

8. Upwork: This is a site where you bid for gigs. Some writers love it, some hate it.

9. Studio D: The editors tend to be picky, but you can write for some big companies through this site.

10. Crowd Content: This site works with big companies like Best Buy.

11. BKA Content: You must be able to write 2,000 words a week to be a member of this site.

12. Internet Marketing Ninjas: No experience necessary to join this team. They will train you.

13. Zen Content: This company was bought by IZEA, a company I have worked with before.

14. Ebyline: Here is another IZEA property.

15. CrowdFlower: You complete simple tasks and get paid. It's a crowdsourcing site.

16. Express Writers: Great site for writers who know what content marketing means.

17. Editor Group: Accepts editors and writers.

18. Content Writers: 50% of every project payment goes to the writer.

19. Content Cavalry: They are looking for looking for specialists in business, automotive, content marketing, fashion, grooming, health, nutrition and fitness.

20. Writology: You can do client work and sell your own articles on this site.

21. ClearVoice: "Our ClearVoice platform matches clients' assignments with freelancers based on industry, pay rates and experience," the website notes.

22. Zerys: This site tends to have a lot of quick freelance gigs.

23. WriterAccess: Super easy place to make a few bucks.

24. Mediashower: They have, "Opportunities to advance to senior-level editorial positions."

25. CopyPress: Pay rates are $.04-$.06/word. Not great, but if the work is quick, you may make some cash.

26. Constant Content: "We currently work with brands like Sport Chek, zulily, The

Brick, CVS, Walgreens and more," they say on their website.

27. <u>Pitchwhiz</u>: A database full of the latest content calls from some of the biggest publications with the ability to send direct messages to the editors.

28. <u>Listverse</u>: Pays $100 per listicle (list-based article).

29. <u>WordApp</u>: Haven't tried this one, so if you have, tell us about it in the comments.

30. <u>WittyPen</u>: "On an average, the writers in Starter level are paid Rs 1/word. We pay flat pricing for each content piece you write with an average word limit," their website says.

31. <u>Content Hourlies</u>: The pay isn't close to great, but if you're fast it may be worth it...maybe...

32. <u>Pitchwiz</u>: Editors post their needs to the site and you can sort through to find websites or magazines that need your work. The dashboard offers you some gigs you may be interested in, or you can target certain niches and markets to create a custom search. There are really quality gigs at Pitchwiz.

Need more help finding clients and gigs?

My book <u>The Fluff-Free Freelance Writing Master Course</u> teaches you how I make $100 to $200 an hour freelance writing from home with real, actionable tips. It is available now on Amazon.

Where to Find Me

- Alinabradford.com
- twitter.com/alinabradford
- facebook.com/nofluffwriter
- medium.com/@alinabradford
- pinterest.com/alinabradford
- instagram.com/nofluffwriter
- linkedin.com/in/alinabradford

Don't forget to join the No-Fluff Freelance Writing Group on Facebook!